Things On Wheels

Contents

Mountain bike

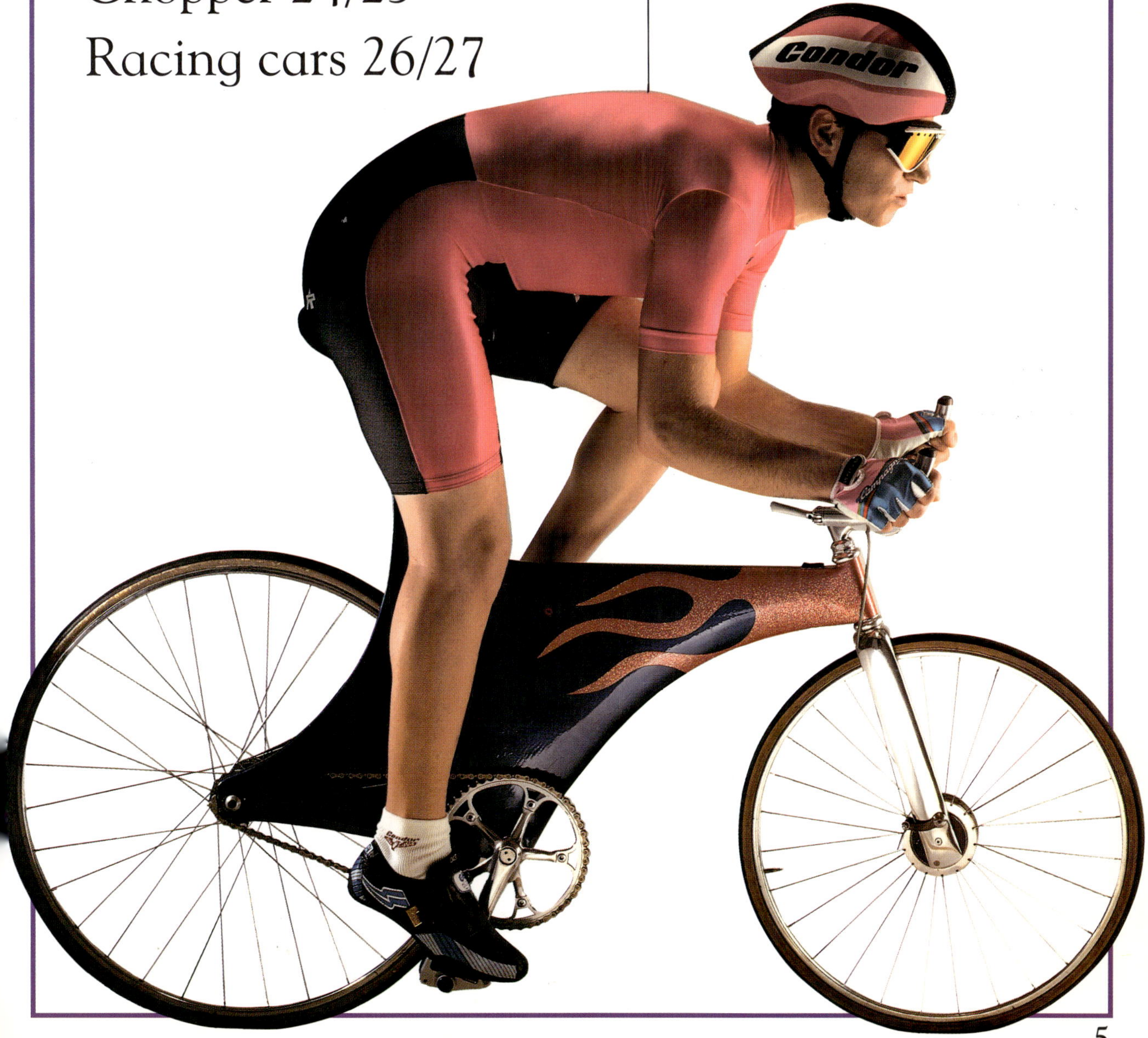

Condor

Where would we be without wheels?

Not very far. Before wheels were invented, walking and horse power were the only means of transport.

When were cars invented?

Cars were invented over a hundred years ago. Early cars look very different from the sleek cars you see today.

Which car would

Nowadays, cars come in many shapes and sizes. Some are brightly painted,

you like to drive?

speedy and fun to drive. Others are comfortable, expensive and luxurious.

What do dumpers do?

They move giant loads, like earth and gravel, and then dump them to make roads and tunnels.

What must you do

Keep your balance! Never forget to follow the rules of the road and always wear a safety hat.

to ride a bicycle?

Bicycles were invented in Europe around 200 years ago. Some bikes are made for two or three riders.

Is this a car?

No, it's a "recumbent" bicycle. The rider takes it easy lying back and peddling at the same time.

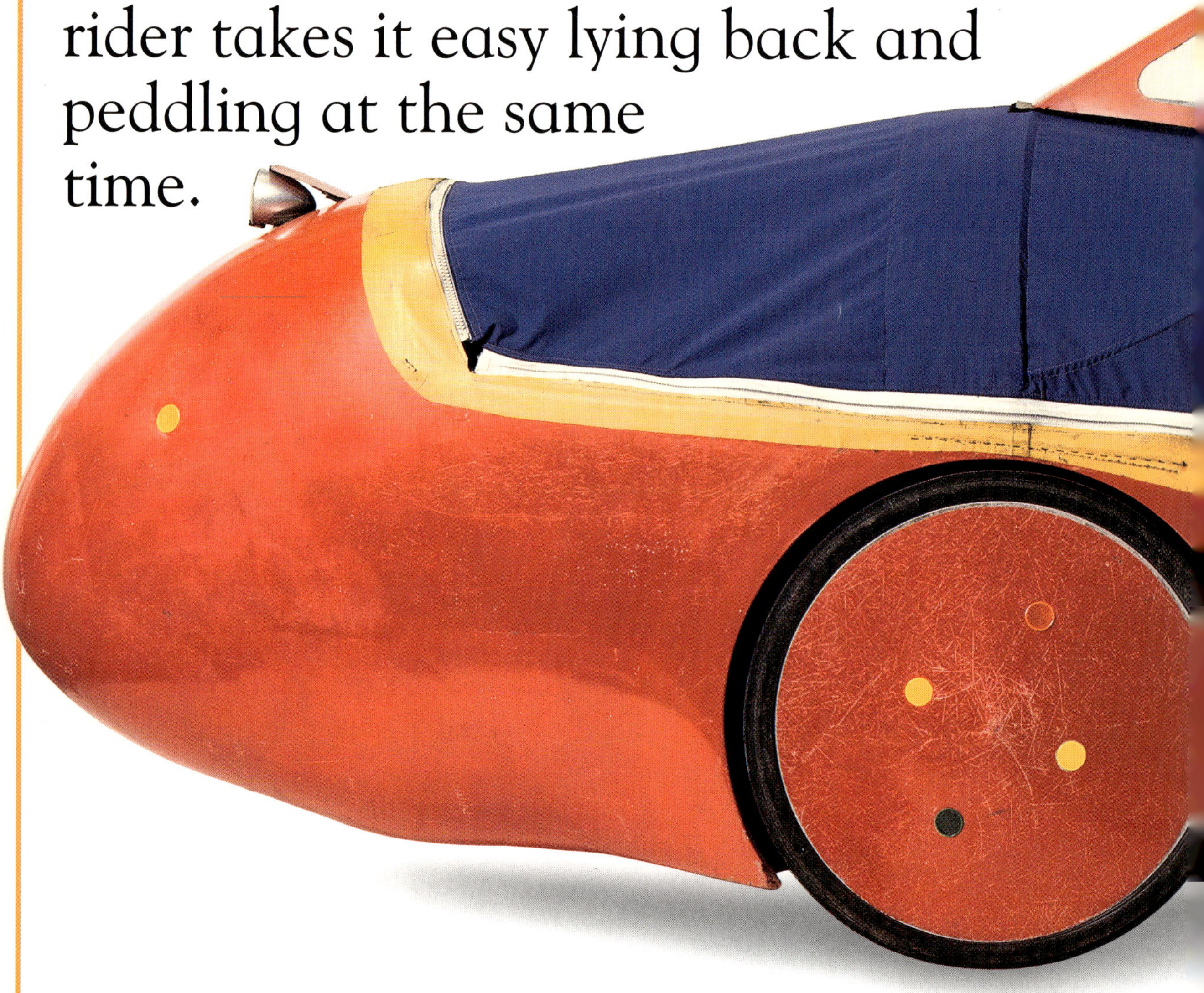

VETTA
Fibre Products
Windcheetah

How many mirrors?

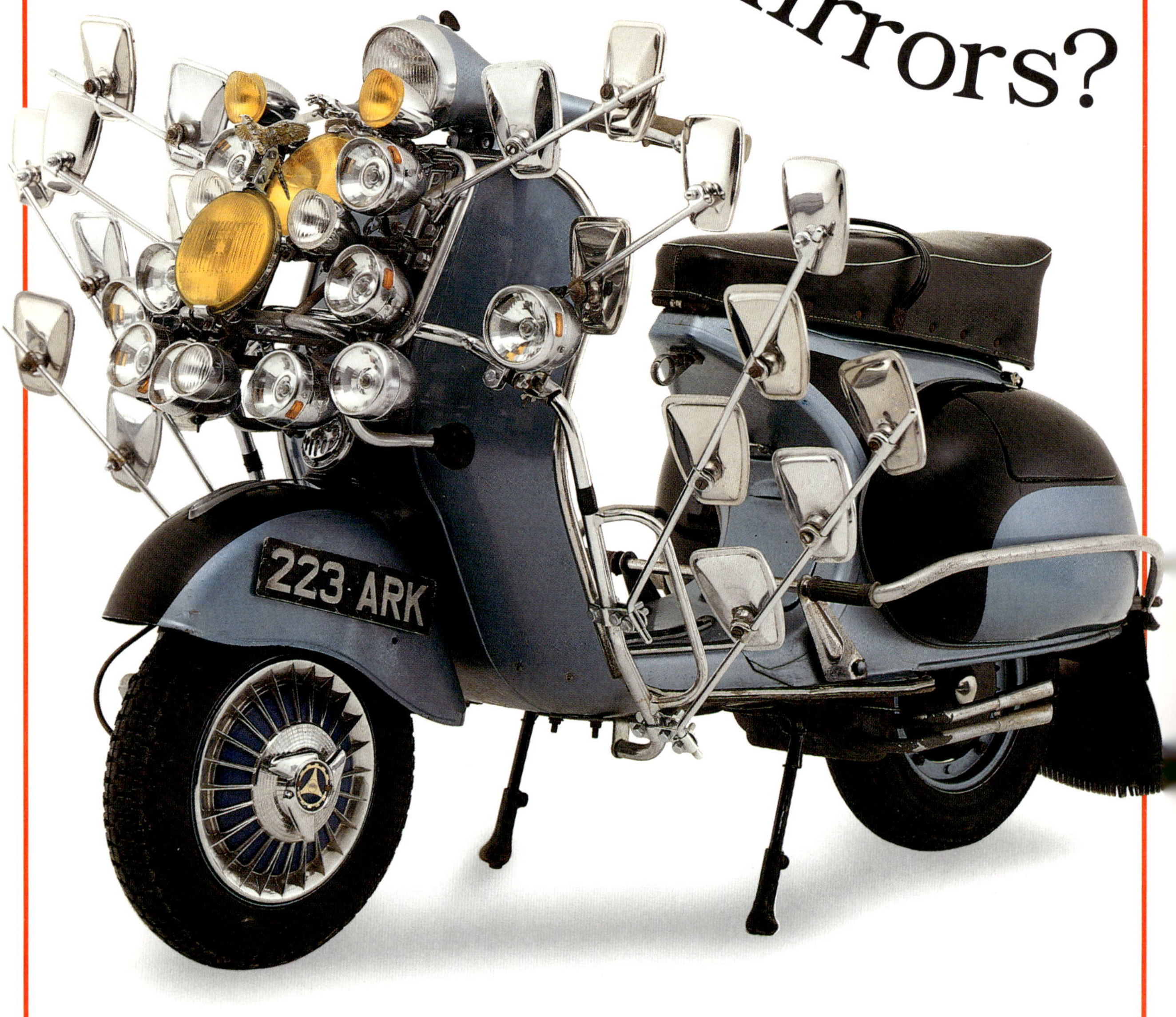

Some people like to decorate their scooters and bikes to make them special. This scooter has 20 mirrors.

Four wheels or two?

Motor bikes have two wheels. They find it easy to weave through the heavy city traffic. This motor bike is the longest in the world. It is 3.8 m (4 yds) long.

What is a city car?

"Minis" are good city cars. They park easily, and carry four passengers, with room for luggage!

"Let's take a taxi!"

This is a London taxi and its yellow light shows it is for hire.

How fast

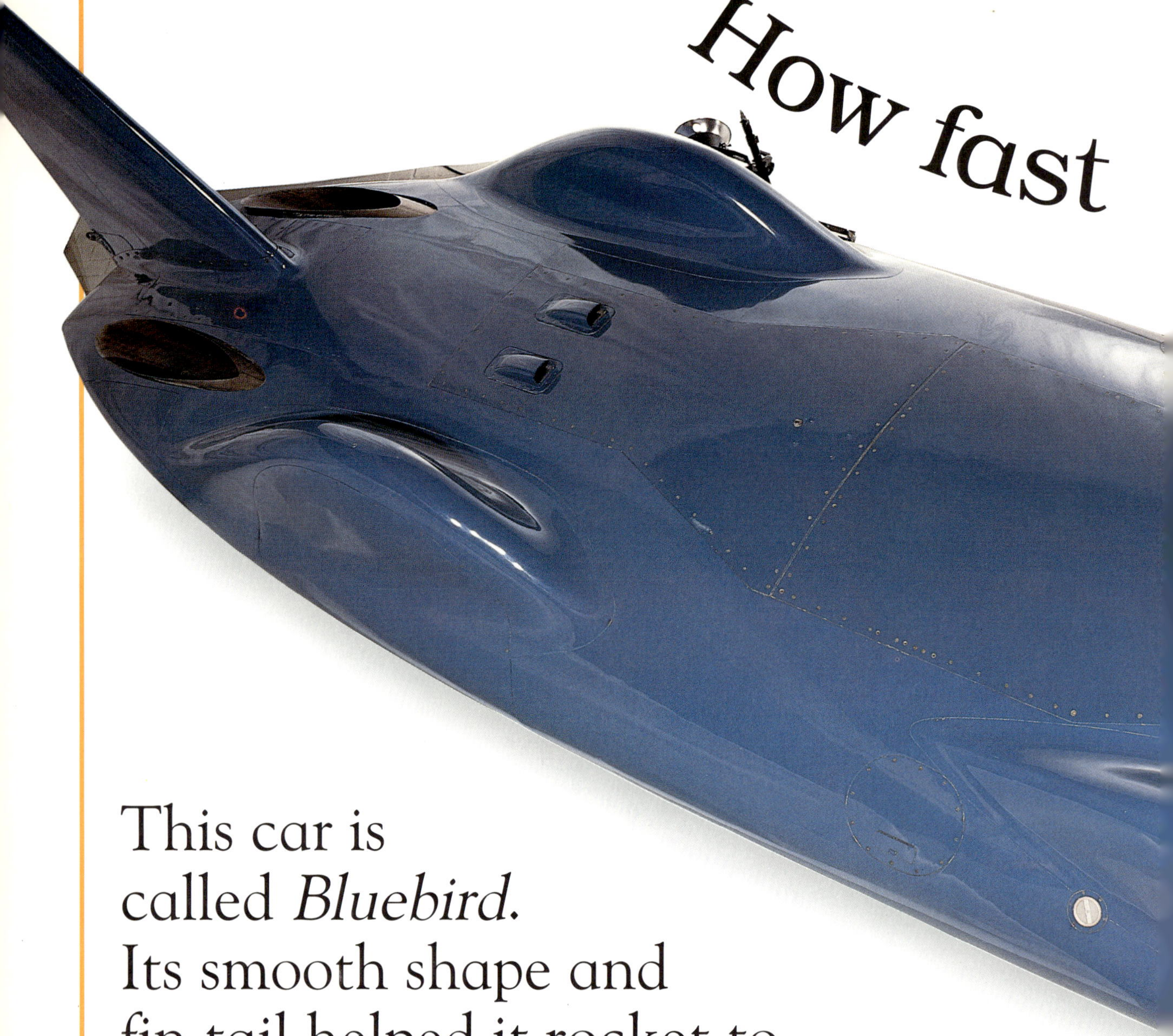

This car is called *Bluebird.* Its smooth shape and fin tail helped it rocket to amazing speeds. In 1964, it zoomed to 648.72 kmph (403.1 mph), setting a land speed record.

is a Bluebird?

What do

The silver engine carries passengers on long trips in its double-decker compartments. The green engine tugs heavy loads like coal, oil and food in its different wagons.

these trains do?

Why is a chopper called a chopper?

People who are really motorbike crazy "chop" bits off their bikes and add new parts. A chopper has high handlebars called apehangers!

On your marks ...

Formula 1 racing cars are very fast machines, whizzing around tracks at over 300 kmph (190 mph).

get set ... go!

There are upside down wings on the back. They hold the car down and keep it from taking off.

FORD

What does a tractor do?

This blue tractor works on a farm, ploughing fields and sowing seeds. It has huge wheels for crossing muddy land.

Have a ...

This sparkling blue Cadillac was built especially for comfortable cruising. It is

nice drive!

a large, heavy car with lots of room for passengers to enjoy a relaxing drive.

500·121
COMMERCIAL MICH.